The Great Barrier Reef

by Emily Hutchinson
illustrated by L. Yerkes

Harcourt

Orlando   Boston   Dallas   Chicago   San Diego

Visit *The Learning Site!*
www.harcourtschool.com

There are many coral reefs in the world. The largest one is the Great Barrier Reef. It stretches more than 1,200 miles (1,931km) along the coast of northern Australia. Coral reefs can be found only off the coast of an island, or the continent of Australia.

There are three kinds of coral reefs: fringing reefs, barrier reefs, and atolls. The first stage in the formation of a coral reef is the fringing reef. It grows up around an island. A fringing reef is separated from the island by a very narrow strip of shallow water.

Over time, as the island begins to wear away, the growing fringing reef becomes a barrier reef. This happens because the stretch of water that separates the reef from the island grows wider as the island becomes smaller. This body of water is called a lagoon.

The Great Barrier Reef in Australia is only 10 miles (16.093 km) off the coast of the island at its closest point. Yet it is as much as 150 miles (241.395 km) off the coast in other places. The Great Barrier Reef protects the lagoon and the Australian shore from the rough winds and waves of the Coral Sea. The Coral Sea is the name of the body of water on the other side of the Great Barrier Reef. The waters of the lagoon, however, are calm and shallow.

An atoll is a coral island that is usually shaped like a horseshoe. Inside the horseshoe is a shallow lagoon. Atolls often grow in the lagoon that separates a barrier reef from the shoreline. These islands of coral make it difficult to sail a boat in barrier reef lagoons.

Like a barrier reef, an atoll was once attached to an island. The island was the top of an undersea volcano that had risen above the ocean surface. As the volcanic peak was worn away by erosion, it slowly disappeared below the surface. The coral reef that remains, the atoll, looks like a ring-shaped island.

All coral reefs have certain things in common. First, they are all found in tropical ocean waters. The shallow water must not get above 68 degrees Fahrenheit (20 degrees Celsius). Second, all coral reefs look like colorful ridges. Third, all coral reefs are formed by tiny sea animals called coral polyps.

Coral polyps are tiny animals with soft bodies. These animals grow no larger than a human fingernail. Often, they are only the size of a match head. The coral polyp has a body shaped like a tube with tentacles on one end. It uses its tentacles to capture food.

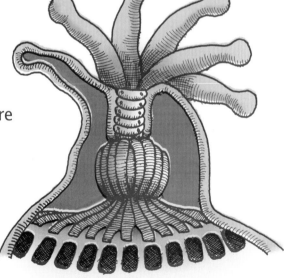

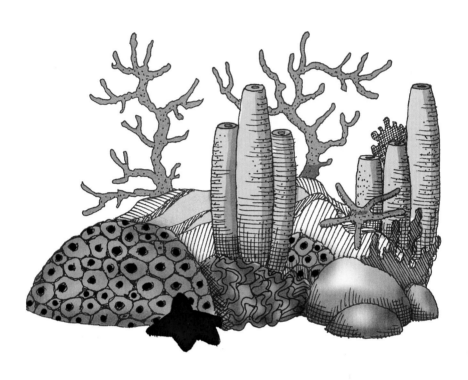

Coral polyps live together in large groups
and are all connected to one another. When
coral polyps die, their skeletons become part
of the coral reef. Other polyps live on top of
these skeletons and then die and leave their
skeletons behind, continuing the cycle. It
takes thousands—even millions—of years to
form a coral reef. Scientists think the Great
Barrier Reef began forming more than
30 million years ago.

The bodies of the living polyps have bright colors of pink, yellow, blue, purple, and green. Scuba divers have said that they look like flower gardens because they are so colorful.

The many fish and other animals and plants also lend color to the Great Barrier Reef. Far from barren, the Great Barrier Reef is home to more than 1,400 species of fish, sponges, and other animals and about 3,500 species of plants.

Imagine what it would be like to go scuba diving on the Great Barrier Reef. You could meander among the coral, looking for interesting creatures. But as you meandered, you would need to be careful not to break any of the coral or step on any stingrays, which hide in the sand. The sharp, poisonous "teeth" on their tails can really hurt!

While scuba diving, you might see the colorful clown fish. This orange, black, and white fish is unusual because it lives among the tentacles of the sea anemone [ə•nem ́ə•nē]. Other fish are stung by these tentacles. However, the clown fish covers itself with a special slime. This slime protects it from the stings of the anemone. The clown fish swims close to the tentacles, eating the leftovers from the anemone's meals.

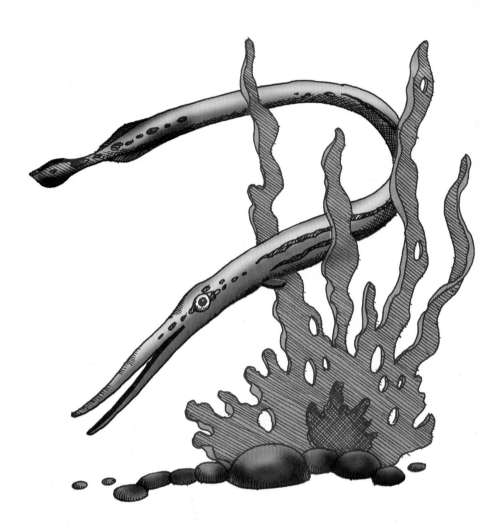

Another colorful fish you might see is the
trumpet fish. Although it eats other fish, it blends
in among fish that are plant-eaters. When smaller
fish come close, it shoots forward suddenly and
eats them. Then it darts into the coral to hide
from its own enemies.

You might also see a fish called the cleaner wrasse. This fish gets its food in a very different way. It nibbles around the mouth and gills of a bigger fish. The bigger fish allows this because by picking off parasites, the wrasse cleans the fish. This helps the bigger fish stay healthy. In return, the wrasse gets a safe meal.

If you go scuba diving at night, look out for the beautiful but deadly lionfish. Its body is covered with poisonous spines. This fish comes out at night, swimming slowly along the reef. It looks for sleeping fish that it can attack.

Another fish you might see at night is the soldier fish. During the day, it lives in caves. During the night, it comes out to feed on the tiny animals and plants that live in the water. The soldier fish has very large eyes that help it see at night.

Another interesting coral reef animal is the sponge. A sponge is an animal that looks something like a plant. It moves water into and out of its holes like a filter as it eats the floating animal plankton.

You might also see the potato cod. This huge fish is sometimes called a grouper. It can grow to be 6 feet long (182.88 cm). What is interesting is that all potato cods are born females. When they grow to full size, they become males.

The Great Barrier Reef, like other coral reefs in the world, is in danger. Unless it is protected, it could turn into a dead and barren place. Sensors from space shuttles have shown how pollution can make the ocean's waters less clear. We know that corals need clear water in order to live.

Pollution, however, is not the only thing harming coral reefs. People who take fish, shells, and coral from the reefs upset the balance of nature.

In 1980, Australia set aside an area of about 4,500 square miles of the reef (1,165,499 ha). It is now against the law to take coral from there. This area, known as the Great Barrier Reef Marine Park, is protected for the future.

The Great Barrier Reef is an amazing sight. The beautiful colors of the coral, as well as the unusual plants and marine animals, make Australia's northern coast a popular place for travelers. One day, you may have a chance to visit this miracle of nature. We should continue to do everything possible to protect this beautiful area of the world.